THE SPIRITUAL COUPLETS
OF
MAULANA JALALU-'D-DIN
MUHAMMAD RUMI

Abridged and Translated

E.H. Whinfield

Masnavi
Book 4

[ZHINGOORA BOOKS]

THE SPIRITUAL COUPLETS
OF
MAULANA JALALU-'D-DIN MUHAMMAD RUMI

Book IV.

STORY I.
The Lover and his Mistress.

THE fourth book begins with an address to Husamu-'d-Din, and this is followed by the story of the lover and his mistress, already commenced in the third book. A certain lover had been separated from his mistress for the space of seven years, during which he never relaxed his efforts to find her. At last his constancy and perseverance were rewarded, in accordance with the promises "The seeker shall find," and "Whoso shall have wrought an atom's weight of good shall behold it." 1 One night, as he was wandering through the city, he was pursued by the patrol, and, in order to escape them, took refuge in a garden, where he found his long-sought mistress. This occasioned him to reflect how often men "hate the things that are good for them," 2 and led him to bless the rough patrol who had procured him the bliss of meeting with his mistress.

Apropos of this, an anecdote is told of a preacher who was in the habit of blessing robbers and oppressors, because their evil example had turned him to righteousness. The moment the lover found himself alone with his mistress, he attempted to embrace her, but his mistress repulsed him, saying, that though no men 'were present, yet the wind was blowing and that showed that God, the mover of the wind, was also present. The lover replied, "It may be I am lacking in good manners, but I am not lacking in constancy and fidelity towards you." His mistress replied, "One must judge of the hidden by the manifest; I see for myself that your outward behavior is bad, and thence I cannot but infer that your boast of hidden virtues is not warranted by actual facts. You are ashamed to misconduct yourself in the sight of men, but have no scruple to do so in the presence of the All-seeing God, and hence I doubt the existence of the virtuous sentiments which you claim to possess, but which can only be known to yourself." To illustrate this, she told the story of a Sufi and his faithless wife. This wife was one day entertaining a paramour, when she was surprised by the sudden return of her husband. On the spur of the moment she threw a woman's dress over her paramour and presented him to her husband as a rich lady who had come to propose a marriage between her son and the Sufi's daughter, saying she did not care for wealth, but only regarded modesty and rectitude of conduct. To this the Sufi replied, that as from her coming unattended it was plain that the lady had not the wealth she pretended to have, it was more than probable that her pretensions to extraordinary modesty and humility were also fictitious. The lover then proceeded to excuse himself by the plea that he had wished to test his mistress, and ascertain for himself whether she was a modest woman or not. He said he of course knew beforehand that she would prove to be a modest woman, but still he wished to have ocular demonstration of the fact. His mistress reproved him for trying to deceive her with false pretences, assuring him that, after he had been detected in a fault, his only proper course was to confess it, as Adam had done. Moreover, she added that an attempt to put her to the test would have been an extremely unworthy proceeding, only to be paralleled by Abu Jahl's attempt to prove the truth of the Prophet's claims by calling on him to perform a miracle.

The soul of good in things evil. Evil only relative.
The lover invoked blessings on that rough patrol,
Because their harshness had wrought bliss for him.
They were poison to most men, but sweets to him,
Because those harsh ones had united him with his love.
In the world there is nothing absolutely bad;
Know, moreover, evil is only relative.
In the world there is neither poison nor antidote,
Which is not a foot to one and a fetter to another;
To one the power of moving, to another a clog;
To one a poison, to another an antidote.
Serpents' poison is life to serpents,
In relation to mankind it is death.
To the creatures of the sea the sea is a garden,

To the creatures of the land it is fatal.
In the same way, O man, reckon up with intelligence
The relations of these things in endless variety.
In relation to this man Zaid is as Satan,
In relation to another he is as a Sultan.
The latter calls Zaid a sincere Mussulman,
The former calls him a Gueber deserving to be killed.
Zaid, one and the same person, is life to the one,
And to the other an annoyance and a pest.
If you desire that God may be pleasing to you,
Then look at Him with the eyes of them that love Him.
Look not at that Beauty with your own eyes,
Look at that Object of desire with His votaries' eyes;
Shut your own eyes from beholding that sweet Object,
And borrow from His admirers their eyes;
Nay, borrow from Him both eyes and sight,
And with those eyes of His look upon His face,
In order that you may not be disappointed with the sight.
God says, "Whoso is God's, God also is his."
God says, "I am his eye, his hand, his heart," 3
That his good fortune may emerge from adversity.
Whatsoever is hateful to you, if it should lead you
To your beloved, at once becomes agreeable to you.
Why God is named "Hearing," "Seeing" and "Knowing".
God calls himself "Seeing," to the end that
His eye may every moment scare you from sinning.
God calls himself "Hearing," to the end that
You may close your lips against foul discourse.
God calls himself "Knowing," to the end that
You may be afraid to plot evil.
These names are not mere accidental names of God,
As a negro may be called Kafu'r (white);
They are names derived from God's essential attributes,
Not mere vain titles of the First Cause.
For if so, they would be only empty pleasantries,
Like calling the deaf a hearer and the blind a seer,

Or a name like "impudent" for a modest man,
Or "beautiful" for an ugly negro,
Or such a title as "Haji" for a new-born boy,
Or that of "Ghazi" applied to a noble idler.
If such titles as these are used in praising persons
Who do not possess the qualities implied, 'tis wrong;
'Twould be jesting or mockery or madness.
"God is exalted above" what is said by evil men. 4
I knew you before I met you face to face;
That you had a fair face but an evil heart;
Yea, I knew you before I saw you,
That you were rooted in iniquity through guile.
When my eye is red owing to inflammation,
I know 'tis so from the pain, though I see it not.
You regarded me as a lamb without a shepherd;
You fancied that I had no guardian.
Lovers have suffered chastisement for this cause,
That they have cast ill-timed looks at fair ones.
They have supposed the fawn to have no shepherd,
They have supposed the captive to be going a begging;
Till in the twinkling of an eye an arrow pierces them,
Saying, "I am her guardian; look not at her rashly!"
What! am I less than a lamb or a fallow deer,
That I should have none to shepherd me?
Nay, I have a Guardian worthy of dominion,
Who knows every wind that blows upon me.
He is aware whether that wind is chill or mild,
He is not ignorant nor absent, O mean one.
The carnal soul is made by God blind and deaf;
I saw with the heart's eye your blindness afar off.
For this cause I never inquired about you for eight years
Because I saw you filled with ignorance and duplicity.
Why indeed should I inquire about one in the furnace,
Who is bowed down with reproach, like yourself?
Comparison of the world to a bath stove,
and of piety to the hot bath.

The lust of the world is like a bath stove,
Whereby the bath of piety is heated;
But the lot of the pious is purity from the stove's filth,
Because they dwell in the bath and in cleanliness.
The rich are as those that carry dung
To heat the furnace of the bath withal.
God has instilled into them cupidity,
That the bath may be warmed and pleasant.
Quit this stove and push on into the bath;
Know quitting the stove to be the bath itself.
Whoso is in the stove-room is as a servant
To him who is temperate and prudent.
Your lust is as fire in the world,
With a hundred greedy mouths wide open.
In the judgment of reason this gold is foul dung,
Although, like dung, it serves to kindle the fire.
Whoso was born in the stove-room and never saw purity,
The smell of sweet musk is disagreeable to him.
In illustration of this, a story follows of a tanner who was
accustomed to bad smells in the course of his trade, and who was
half killed by the smell of musk in the bazaar of the perfumers, but
was cured by the accustomed smell of dung.
*NOTES:
1. Koran xcix. 7.
2. Koran ii. 213.
3. "My servant draws nigh to me by pious deeds till I love him, and,
when I love him, I am his eye, his ear, his tongue, his foot, his hand,
and by me he sees, hears, talks, walks, and feels." Hadis.
4. Cp. Koran xvi 3.

STORY II.

The Building of the "Most Remote Temple" at Jerusalem.
King David purposed to build a temple at Jerusalem, but was
forbidden to do so by a divine voice, because he had been a man of
blood. But, it was added, the work should be accomplished by his
son Solomon, and Solomon's work would be reckoned the same as
David's, in accordance with the texts, "The faithful are brethren,"
and "Sages are as a single soul," and "We make no distinction
between any of the apostles." 1 Accordingly, when Solomon came
to the throne, he set about the building, which was attended with
many miraculous circumstances, e.g., the stones in the quarry
crying out and moving of themselves to the site of the temple.
Bilqis, Queen of Saba, sent Solomon a present of forty camels laden
with ingots of gold; but Solomon would not receive them, and sent
her messengers back with a letter commanding her to abandon the
worship of the sun and embrace Islam. 2 At the same time he
charged the messengers to report fully to the Queen all they had
seen in his kingdom, and to urge her to comply with his commands
to renounce her sovereignty and present herself in all humility at his
court. As she delayed to come, Solomon again sent to assure her
that he had no sinister views regarding her, and desired her
attendance at his court solely for her own spiritual benefit. At last
Bilqis renounced her royal state and cast away all care for worldly
things, and, impelled by earnest desire to learn the true faith,
presented herself at the court of King Solomon. Then Solomon
commanded that the throne of Bilqis should be brought from Saba,
and an 'Afrit offered to fetch it, but Asaf, the vizier anticipated him.
3 Afterwards Solomon proceeded with the building of the temple,
wherein he was assisted by devils and fairies. Then God tried
Solomon by placing on his throne a false counterpart of him. His
miracle working signet was stolen by a devil named Sakhar who
thereupon assumed his shape and personated him for forty days,
during which Solomon had to wander about and beg his bread.

After this he regained his throne, and having completed the temple, began to worship therein. One day he observed that a tuft of coarse grass had sprung up in a corner of the temple, and he was greatly distressed because he thought it portended the ruin of the building, but he took comfort from the thought that while he himself lived the temple would not be allowed to fall into ruin; so long as he lived, at least, he would root up all evil weeds that threatened the safety of the temple, as well the temple built with hands as the spiritual temple in his heart.

In the course of this story, which is told at great length, there occur anecdotes of the beginning of the reign of 'Othman, of the miracles of 'Abdullah Moghrabi, and others, of which abstracts are given below.

Though philosophers call man the microcosm, divines call him the macrocosm.

In outward form thou art the microcosm,
But in reality the macrocosm. 4
Seemingly the bough is the cause of the fruit, 5
But really the bough exists because of the fruit.
Were he not impelled by desire of fruit,
The gardener would never have planted the tree.
Therefore in reality the tree is born from the fruit,
Though seemingly the fruit is born from the tree.
For this cause Mustafa said, "Adam and all prophets
Are my followers and gather under my standard.
Though to outward view I am a son of Adam,
In reality I am his first forefather,
Because the angels worshipped him for my sake,
And 'twas in my footsteps that he ascended to heaven.
Hence in reality our first parent was my offspring,
As in reality the tree is born of its own fruit."
What is first in thought is last in act.
Thought is the special attribute of the Eternal.
This product goes forth from heaven very swiftly,
And comes to us like a caravan. 6
'Tis not a long road that this caravan travels;

Can the desert stop the deliverer?
The heart travels to the Ka'ba every moment,
And by divine grace the body acquires the same power.
Distance and nearness affect only the body,
What do they matter in the place where God is?
When God changes the body,
It regards not parasangs or miles.
Even on earth there is hope of approaching God.
Press on like a lover, and cease vain words, O son!
In the course of his rebuke to the messengers of Bilqis for bringing
him mere gold instead of a humble heart, Solomon tells the story of
the druggist who used soapstone or Persian earth for a weight. A
man came to him to buy sugar-candy, and as he had no weight at
hand, he used a lump of soapstone instead; but, while his back was
turned, the purchaser stole a bit of the soapstone. The druggist,
though he saw what he was doing, would not interrupt him, for he
knew that the more soapstone the purchaser stole, the less sugar-
candy he would get. In like manner the more men grasp at the
transitory wealth of this world, the less they will obtain of the stable
wealth of the world to come.
Part of Soloman's message to Bilqis.
Report to Bilqis what marvels ye have seen,
And what plains of gold belong to Solomon;
How ye beheld forty mansions faced with gold,
And how ye were ashamed of your presents;
That she may know Solomon is not covetous of gold;
He has received gold from the Creator of gold.
The moment he wills it, every grain of earth's dust
Is changed into gold and precious pearls.
For this cause, O thou that lovest gold,
On the last day God will make earth all silver (white). 7
Quit thy wealth, even if it be the realm of Saba;
Thou wilt find many realms not of this earth.
What thou callest a throne is only a prison;
Thou thinkest thyself enthroned, but art outside the door.
Thou hast no sovereignty over thine own passions,

How canst thou sway good and evil?
Thy hair turns white without thy concurrence,
Take shame to thyself for thy evil passions.
Whoso bows his head to the King of kings
Will receive a hundred kingdoms not of this world;
But the delight of bowing down before God
Will seem sweeter to thee than countless glories."
An anecdote follows of a darvesh who saw in a dream some saints, and prayed them to provide him with his daily bread without obliging him to mix in worldly affairs. The saints ordered him to go to the forest, and there he found that all the wild fruits were rendered fit for his food. Having a few grains of gold by him, which he had gained by worldly labour before this miracle had been wrought for him, he was about to give them to a poor woodcutter who was passing that way. But this woodcutter was a saint, and at once read his thoughts, and to show, like Solomon, that he had no need of worldly wealth, he offered up a short prayer to God, and straightway his bundle of firewood was changed into gold, and immediately after, at another prayer, was changed back again into firewood.

Ibrahim bin Adham aud his fondness for music. 8

Haste to renounce thy kingdom, like Ibrahim bin Adham,
To obtain, like him, the kingdom of eternity.
At night that king would sleep on his throne,
With his guards of state surrounding his palace,
Though he needed no guards for the purpose
Of warding off robbers and vagabonds;
For he who is a just king knows everything,
And is safe from harm and his mind is at peace.
Justice is the guardian of his steps,
Not guards with drums round his palace.
His purpose in having this band of music was this,
To recall to his longing heart that call of God. 9
The wailing of horn and the thunder of drum

Resemble in some sort that dread "trumpet blast." 10
Wherefore philosophers say that we have learned
Our melodies from those of the revolving spheres.
The song of the spheres in their revolutions
Is what men sing with lute and voice.
The faithful hold that the sweet influences of heaven
Can make even harsh voices melodious.
As we are all members of Adam,
We have heard these melodies in Paradise;
Though earth and water have cast their veil upon us,
We retain faint reminiscences of those heavenly songs.
But while we are thus shrouded by gross earthly veils,
How can the tones of the dancing spheres reach us? 11
Hence it is that listening to music is lovers' food,
Because it recalls to them their primal union with God.
The inward feelings of the mind acquire strength,
Nay, are shown outwardly, under influence of music.
The fire of love burns hotter under stimulus of music,
Even as occurred in the case of the nut-gatherer.
Ibrahim's abdication.
Once that noble Ibrahim, as he sat on his throne,
Heard a clamour and noise of cries on the roof,
Also heavy footsteps on the roof of his palace.
He said to himself, "Whose heavy feet are those?"
He shouted from his window, "Who goes there?
'Tis no man's step; surely 'tis a fairy."
His guards, filled with confusion, bowed their heads,
Saying, "It is we who are going the rounds in search."
He said, "What seek ye?" They said "Our camels" 12
He said, "Who ever searched for camels on a housetop?"
They said, "We follow thy example,
Who seekest union with God while sitting on a throne."
This was all, and no man ever saw him again,
Just as fairies are invisible to men.
His substance was hid from men, though he was with them,
For what can men see save the outward aspect and dress?

As he was removed from the sight of friends and strangers,
His fame was noised abroad like that of the 'Anka.
For the soul of every bird that reaches Mount Qaf
Confers glory on the whole family of birds. 13
The anecdote of the nut-gatherer, introduced in the above story, is
only another version of the story of the thirsty man who threw
bricks into the water in order to hear the sound of the splash. 14
This is followed by an address to Husamu-'d-Din, in which the poet
says that his object in writing the Masnavi was to elicit words from
Husam, as his words were the same as the words of God.
Solomon's preaching to the people of Bilqis. The art of preaching.
I tell the tale of Saba in lovers' style.
When the breeze bore Solomon's words to that garden,
'Twas as when bodies meet souls at the resurrection,
Or as when boys return to their loved homes.
The people of love are hidden amongst the peoples,
As a liberal man encompassed by the contumely of the base.
Souls are disgraced by union with bodies,
Bodies are ennobled by union with souls.
Arise, O lovers; this sweet draught is yours;
Ye are they that endure; eternal life is yours.
Ho! ye that seek, arise and take your fill of love,
Snuff up that perfume of Yusuf!
Approach, O Solomon, thou that knowest birds' language,
Sound the note of every bird that draws near; 15
When God sent, thee to the birds,
He taught thee first the notes of all the birds.
To the predestinarian bird talk predestination,
To the bird with broken wings preach patience,
To the patient well-doer preach comfort and pardon,
To the spiritual 'Anka relate the glories of Mount Qaf,
To the pigeon preach avoidance of the hawk,
To the lordly hawk mercy and self-control;
As for the bat, who lingers helpless in the dark,
Acquaint him with the society of the light;
To the fighting partridge teach peace,

To the cock the signs of dawning day.
In this way deal with all from the hoopoo to the eagle.
Then follows a long account of various miraculous incidents that
occurred during the childhood of the Prophet, how he was suckled
by Halima, a woman of the Bani Sa'ad, how the idols bowed down
before him, how he strayed from home, how his grandfather, Abd
ul Muttalib, prayed to God that he might be found, and how he was
at last found in the Ka'ba and restored to his grandfather.
Next a story is told of a cur who attacked a blind man (Kur) in the
street, rather than hunt the wild ass (Gor) on the mountains in
company with well-bred dogs. This is an illustration of the thesis
that mankind is prone to run after mean earthly objects, and to
neglect aspiring to the spiritual world.
Solomon's admonitions to Bilqis.
Ah! Bilqis, bestir thyself now the market is thronged,
Flee away from them whose traffic is unprofitable! 16
Arise, Bilqis, now that thou hast the choice,
Before that death lays his heavy hand upon thee.
Soon will death pull thy ears, as if thou wert
A thief dragged before the officer in deadly fear.
How long wilt thou steal shoes from asses of the world?
If thou must steal, steal pearls of the world above.
Thy sisters have found the kingdom that lasts forever,
Thou cleavest to the kingdom of darkness.
Happy is he who quits this earthly kingdom,
Which sooner or later death will destroy.
Arise! O Bilqis, at least behold
The kingdom of the royal kings of the faith!
In reality they are seated in the garden of the spirit,
Though to outward view they are guiding their friends.
That spiritual garden accompanies them everywhere,
Yet it is never revealed to the eyes of the people,
Its fruits ever asking to be gathered,
Its fount of life welling up to be drunk!
Go round about the heavens without aid of wings,
Like sun or full moon or new moon!

Thou wilt move as a spirit without aid of feet,
Thou wilt eat sweet viands without mouth or palate.
No crocodile of sorrow will attack thy bark,
Nor will sad thoughts of death assail thee.
Thou wilt be at once queen, army, and throne,
Endued with good fortune and fortune itself. 17
Thou sayest thou art a great queen of good fortune;
But thy fortune is apart from thee and will soon fade,
Thou wilt be left like a, beggar without sustenance;
Therefore, O chosen one, become thy own fortune.
When, O spiritual one, thou hast become thy own fortune,
Then, being thyself thy fortune, thou wilt never lose it.
How. O fortunate one, canst thou ever lose thyself,
When thy real self is thy treasure and thy kingdom?
How men and demons helped Solomon in building the temple.
When Solomon laid the foundations of the temple,
Men and Jinns came and lent their aid to the work,
Some of them with good-will, and others on compulsion,
Even as worshippers follow the road of devotion.
Men are as demons, and lust of wealth their chain,
Which drags them forth to toil in shop and field.
This chain is made of their fears and anxieties.
Deem not that these men have no chain upon them.
It causes them to engage in labor and the chase,
It forces them to toil in mines and on the sea,
It urges them towards good and towards evil.
God saith, "On their necks is a rope of palm fibre," 18
And "Verily on their necks have we placed ropes," 19
"We make this rope out of their own dispositions;
There is none either impure or intelligent,
But we have fastened his work about his neck." 20
Thy lust is even as fire burning in thy evil deeds;
The black coal of these deeds is lighted by the fire;
The blackness of the coal is first hidden by the fire,
But, when it is burnt, the blackness is made visible.
The building of the prophets was without lust,

And accordingly its splendor ever increased.
Yea, many are the noble temples they have raised,
Though all were not named "The Most Remote Temple."
The Ka'ba, whose renown waxes greater every moment,
Owed its foundation to the piety of Abraham.
Its glory is not derived from stones and mortar,
But from being built without lust or strife.
Neither are the prophets' writings like other writings;
Nor their temples, nor their works, nor their families;
Nor their manners, nor their wrath, nor their chastisements;
Nor their dreams, nor their reason, nor their words.
Each one of them is endued with a different glory,
Each soul's bird winged with different feathers.
Ho! pious ones, build the lively temple of the heart,
That the Divine Solomon may be seen, and peace be upon you!
And if your demons and fairies be recalcitrant,
Your good angels must place collars on their necks.
If your demons go astray through guile and fraud,
Chastisement must overtake them swift as lightning.
Be like Solomon, so that your demons
May dig stones for your spiritual edifice.
Be like Solomon, free from evil thoughts and guile,
So that carnal demons and Jinns may be submissive to you.
Your heart is as Solomon's signet; take good care
That it falls not a prey to demons,
For then demons will rule over you as over Solomon.
Guard then your signet from the demons, and be at peace.
Then follows a story of a poet who recited a panegyric in honor of a
liberal king. The king commanded that he should receive one
thousand pieces of gold, but the vazir, named Abul-Hasan, gave him
ten thousand. The poet went to his home well contented, but after
some years fell into poverty, and naturally bethought him of the
generous king and his vazir, who had before assisted him.
Sibawayh, the grammarian of Shiraz says "Allah" is derived from
"Alah" (fleeing for refuge) and thus we see all creatures, and even
the elements themselves, ever looking to Allah to sustain them in

existence. The poet, therefore, again presented himself to the king with a new panegyric, and the king, on hearing it, commanded as before that a thousand pieces of gold should be given him. But the new vazir, who was also named Abul-Hasan, persuaded the king that the exchequer could not afford this large outlay, and kept the poet waiting so long for his money, that at last he was glad to get away with only one hundred pieces of gold. These two vazirs recall Asaf, the good vazir of King Solomon, who deserves the title "Light upon light," 21 and Haman, the evil vazir of Pharaoh, who turned his he,art against Moses, and brought many plagues upon the kingdom of Egypt.

How all creatures cry to God for sustenance.

Yea, all the fish in the seas,
And all feathered fowl in the air above,
All elephants, wolves, and lions of the forest,
All dragons and snakes, and even little ants,
Yea, even air, water, earth, and fire,
Draw their sustenance from Him, both winter and summer.
Every moment this heaven cries to Him, saying,
"O Lord, quit not Thy hold of me for a moment!
The pillar of my being is Thy aid and protection;
The whole is folded up in that right hand of Thine." 22
And earth cries, "O keep me fixed and steadfast,
Thou who hast placed me on the top of waters!"
All of them are waiting and expecting His aid,
All have learned of Him to represent their needs.
Every prophet extols this prescription,
"Seek ye help with patience and with prayer." 23
Ho! seek aid of Him, not of another than Him
Seek water in the ocean, not in a dried-up channel.

The next anecdote is that of the raven who taught Cain the art of digging graves and burying corpses, as told in Koran v. 34. This is designed to illustrate the thesis that unaided human reason can discover no now truth, unless inspired by Divine wisdom, of which

17

the prophets, and especially "Universal Reason," or the Prophet Muhammed, are the channels. Thus physicians and herbalists have derived their knowledge of the virtues of plants from the instructions originally given by King Solomon when he classified the plants that grew in the court of the temple. The inner eye sees more than is visible to the sight of the vulgar. To illustrate this, an anecdote is told of a Sufi who had accompanied his friends to a beautiful garden, but instead of looking about and enjoying the fragrance of the flowers and fruits, sat with his head sunk on his breast in Sufi fashion. His friends said to him, in the words of the Koran, "Look at the signs of God's mercy, how after its death He quickeneth the earth!" 24 He answered them that these signs were far more plainly visible to him in his heart than in the outward creation, which was merely as it were a blurred reflection from the spiritual creation enshrined in his heart. For God says, "The life of the world is naught but a cheating fruition." 25 In other words, "Nature conceals God, but the supernatural in man reveals Him." 26 On cleansing the inward temple of the heart from self-conceit and reliance on carnal reason.

When the body bows in worship, the heart is a temple,
And where there is a temple, there bad friends are weeds
When a liking for bad friends grows up in you,
Flee from them, and avoid converse with them.
Root up those weeds, for, if they attain full growth,
They will subvert you and your temple together.
O beloved, this weed is deviation from the "right way,"
You crawl crookedly, like infants unable to walk.
Fear not to acknowledge your ignorance and guilt,
That the Heavenly Master may not withhold instruction.
When you say, "I am ignorant; O teach me,"
Such open confession is better than false pride.
O ingenuous one, learn of our father Adam,
Who said of yore, "O Lord, we have dealt unjustly." 27
He made no vain excuses and prevaricated not,
Nor did he raise the standard of guile and craft.
On the other hand, Iblis raised arguments, saying,

"I used to be honorable; Thou hast disgraced me.
My stain is owing to Thee; Thou art my dyer;
Thou hast caused my sin and transgression."
Read the text, "Lord, Thou hast caused me to err," 28
That you plead not compulsion, and so err (like Iblis).
How long will you climb into that tree of compulsion?
How long cast out of sight your own freewill?
How long, like Iblis and his evil crew,
Throw the blame of your own sins upon God?
How were you compelled to sin when you took such pleasure
And pride in engaging in those sins?
Does a man feel such pleasure in acting on compulsion
As he exhibits when committing wrong actions?
You battle like twenty men against those
Who give you good advice not to do that act;
Saying to them, "This is right and quite proper;
Who dissuades me from it but men of no account?"
Does a man acting on compulsion talk like this?
Or rather one who is erring of his own freewill?
Whatever your lust wills you deem freewill,
What reason demands you deem compulsion.
Whoso is wise and prudent knows this,
That cleverness comes from Iblis, but love from Adam.
Cleverness is like Canaan's swimming in the ocean; 29
'Tis no river or small stream; 'tis the mighty ocean.
Away with this attempt to swim; quit self-conceit.
'Twill not save you; Canaan was drowned at last.
Love is as the ark appointed for the righteous,
Which annuls the danger and provides a way of escape.
Sell your cleverness and buy bewilderment;
Cleverness is mere opinion, bewilderment intuition.
Make sacrifice of your reason at the feet of Mustafa,
Say, "God Sufficeth me, for He, is sufficient for me." 30
Do not, like Canaan, hang back from entering the ark,
Being puffed up with vain conceit of cleverness.
He said, "I will escape to the top of high mountains,

Why need I put myself under obligation to Noah?"
Ah! better for him had he never learnt swimming!
Then he would have based his hopes on Noah's ark.
Would he had been ignorant of craft as a babe!
Then like a babe he would have clung to his mother.
Would he had been less full of borrowed knowledge!
Then he would have accepted inspired knowledge from his father.
When, with inspiration at hand, you seek book-learning,
Your heart, as if inspired, loads you with reproach. 31
Traditional knowledge, when inspiration is available,
Is like making ablutions with sand when water is near.
Make yourself ignorant, be submissive, and then
You will obtain release from your ignorance.
For this cause, O son, the Prince of men declared,
"The majority of those in Paradise are the foolish." 32
Cleverness is as a wind raising storms of pride;
Be foolish, so that your heart may be at peace;
Not with the folly that doubles itself by vain babble,
But with that arising from bewilderment at "The Truth."
Those Egyptian women who cut their hands were fools 33
Fools as to their hands, being amazed at Yusuf's face.
Make sacrifice of reason to love of "The Friend,"
True reason is to be found where He is.
Men of wisdom direct their reason heavenwards,
Vain babblers halt on earth where no "Friend" is.
If through bewilderment your reason quits your head,
Every hair of your head becomes true reason and a head.
Then follow commentaries on the text, "O thou enfolded in thy
mantle;" 34 on the proverb, "Silence is the proper answer to a fool;"
on the Hadis, "God created the angels with reason and the brutes
with lust, but man he created with both reason and lust; the man
who follows reason is higher than the angels, and the man who
follows lust is lower than the brutes;" on the text, "As to those in
whose heart is a disease, it will add doubt to their doubt, and they
shall die infidels," 35 and a comparison of the struggle between
reason and lust to that between Majnun and his she-camel, he

20

trying to get to his mistress Laila, and the she-camel trying to run home to her foal.

*NOTES:

1. Koran xlix. 10; xxxi. 27; ii. 285.

2. The letter is given in Koran xxvii. 30.

3. All these legends are derived from Koran xxi., xxvii., and xxxviii. See Sale's notes.

4. This refers to Muhammad, who is at once the "First reason" (Logos) and the "Perfect man," who is "the sum of all the worlds" and the "Great world." See Notices et Extraits des MSS., x. p. 86.

5. He was also the final cause of creation. "If it had not been for thee, the world had not been created."

6. Muhammad as the Logos is the channel by which divine grace is conveyed to man. The "change of the body" is an allusion to the ascension of Muhammad (Mi raj).

7. A Hadis.

8. Music is much used in the religious services of the "Maulavi" order of Darveshes, founded by Jalalu -d-Din Rumi. See "The Dervishes," by J.P. Brown, p. 197.

9. "Am not I your lord?" (Koran vii. 171).

10. "When there shall be a trumpet blast, that shall be a dreadful day" (Koran lxxiv. 7).

11. The so-called Pythagorean doctrine of the "Harmony of the spheres" was as well known to Persian poets as to Shakespeare.

12. This is an allusion to the story of the "Believer's lost camel." Book ii., Story xi.

13. This alludes to the well-known poem of Faridu-d-Din 'Attar the "Mantiqu-t-Tair."

14. Book ii. Story v.

15. Koran xxvii. 16. There is a Hadis, "Speak to men according to the amount of their intelligence."

16. "These are they who have bought error at the price of guidance, but their traffic hath not been gainful" (Koran ii. 15).

17. Union attained, all duality and separate phenomenal existence are swallowed up in the One (Noumenon). (See Gulshan i Raz, I. 835 and 845).

18. Koran iii. 5.

19. Koran xxxvi. 7.

20. "And every man's work have we fastened about his neck, and on the last day will we bring forth to him a book, which shall be shown to him wide open. Read thy book; there needeth none but thyself to make out an account against thee that day " (Koran xvii. 14).

21. Koran xxiv. 35.

22. Koran xxxix. 67.

23. Koran ii. 148.

24. Koran xxx. 49.

25. Koran iii. 182.

26. "But is it unreasonable to confess that we believe in God, not by reason of the nature which conceals him, but by reason of the supernatural in man, which alone reveals him and proves him to exist? " (Jacobi, quoted in Sir W. Hamilton's Lectures on Metaphysics, vol. i. p. 40).

27. Koran vii. 22.

28. He said, "That thou hast caused me to err" (Koran vii. 15). This is the burden of many of 'Omar Khayyam's poems.

29. Koran xi. 43. See Book iii., Story 5.

30. Koran ix. 130.

31. Knowledge of "The Truth" is to be attained not by exercise of the reason, but by illumination from above. When the light of "The Truth" is revealed, reason is drowned in bewilderment. Gulshan i Raz, Answer ii.

32. Freytag, Arabum Proverbia, vol. ii. p. 898; 1 Cor. iv. 10.

33. "They were amazed at Yusuf, and cut their hands, and said, 'God keep us, this is no man!'" (Koran xii. 31).

34. Koran lxxiii. 1.

35. Koran ix. 126.

STORY III.

The Youth who wrote a letter of complaint
about his rations to the King.
A certain youth in the service of a great king was dissatisfied with
his rations, so he went to the cook and reproached him with
dishonoring his master by his stinginess. The youth would not listen
to his excuses, but wrote off an angry letter of complaint to the
king, in terms of outward compliment and respect, but betraying an
angry spirit. On receiving this letter, the king observed that it
contained only complaints about meat and drink, and evinced no
aspirations after spiritual food, and therefore needed no answer, as
"the proper answer to a fool is silence." 1 When the youth received
no answer to his letter, he was much surprised, and threw the
blame on the cook and on the messenger, ignoring the fact that the
folly of his own letter was the real reason of its being left
unanswered. He wrote in all five letters, but the king persisted in his
refusal to reply, saying that fools are enemies to God and man, and
that he who has any dealings with a fool fouls his own nest. Fools
only regard material meat and drink, whereas the food of the wise
is the light of God, as it is said by the Prophet, "I pass the night in
the presence of my Lord, who giveth me meat and drink," 2 and
again, "Fasting is the food of God," i.e., the means by which spiritual
food is obtained. 3
Explanation of the text "And Moses conceived a secret fear within
him. We said 'Fear not, for thou shalt be uppermost (over Pharaoh's
magicians) '". 4
Moses said, "Their sorcery confuses them;
What can I do? These people have no discernment."
God said, "I will generate in them discernment;
I will make their undiscerning reason to see clearly.
Although like a sea their waves cast up foam,
O Moses, thou shalt prevail over them; fear not!"
The magicians gloried in their own achievements,

But when Moses' rod became a snake, they were confounded.
Whoso boasts of his beauty and wit,
The stone of death is a touchstone of his boasts.
Sorcery fades away, but the miracles of Moses advance.
Both resemble a dish falling from a roof:
The noise of the dish of sorcery leaves only cursing;
The noise of the dish of faith leaves edification.
When the touchstone is hidden from the sight of all,
Then come forth to battle and boast, O base coin!
Your time for boasting is when the touchstone is away;
The hand of power will soon crush your exaltation.
The base coin says to me with pride every moment,
"O pure gold, how am I inferior to you?"
The gold replies, "Even so, O comrade;
But the touchstone is at hand; be ready to meet it!"
Death of the body is a benefaction to the spiritual;
What damage has pure gold to dread from the shears?
If the base coin were of itself far-sighted,
It would reveal at first the blackness it shows at last.
If it had showed its blackness at first on its face,
'Twould have avoided hypocrisy now and misery at last.
'Twould have sought the alchemy of grace in due time;
Its reason would have prevailed over its hypocrisy.
If it became broken-hearted through its own bad state,
'Twould look onward to Him that heals the broken;
'Twould look to the result and be broken-hearted
And be made whole at once by the Healer of broken hearts.
Divine grace places base copper in the alembic,
Adulterated gold is excluded from that favor.
O adulterated gold, boast not, but see clearly
That thy Purchaser is not blind to thy defects.
The light of the judgment-day will enlighten his eyes
And destroy the glamour of thy fascinations.
Behold them that have regard to the ultimate result,
And also the regrets of foolish souls and their envy.
Behold them that regard only the present,

And cast away thoughts of evil to come from their minds.

*NOTES:

1. See Freytag, Arabum Proverbia, i. 551, for a parallel.
2. Koran xxvi. 79.
3. See Mishkat ul Masabih, vol. i. p. 463.
4. Koran xx. 70.

STORY IV.

Bayazid and his impious sayings when beside himself.
The holy saint Bayazid before his death predicted the birth of the saint Abul-Hasan Khirqani, and specified all the peculiar qualities which would be seen in him. And after his death it came to pass as he had predicted, and Abul-Hasan, hearing what Bayazid had said, used to frequent his tomb. One day he visited the tomb as usual, and found it covered with snow, and a voice was heard saying, "The world is fleeting as snow. I am calling thee! Follow me and forsake the world!"
How Bayazid cried out, when beside himself, "Glory be to me!" and how his disciples were scandalized at this saying, and how Bayazid answered them.

Once that famous saint Bayazid came to his disciples,
Saying, "Lo, I myself am God Almighty."
That man of spiritual gifts being visibly beside himself;
Said, "There is no God beside me; worship me!"
Next morning, when his ecstatic state had passed,
They said, "You said so and so, which was impious."
He answered, "If I do so again,
Straightway slay me with your knives!
God is independent of me; I am in the body.
If I say that again you must kill me!"
When that holy person had given this injunction,
Each of his disciples made ready his knife.
Again that overflowing cup became beside himself,
And his recent injunctions passed from his mind.
Alienation came upon him, reason went astray,
The dawn shone forth and his lamp paled at its light.
Reason is like an officer when the king appears;
The officer then loses his power and hides himself.

Reason is God's shadow; God is the sun.
What power has the shadow before the sun?
When a man is possessed by an evil spirit
The qualities of humanity are lost in him.
Whatever he says is really said by that spirit,
Though it seems to proceed from the man's mouth.
When the spirit has this rule and dominance over him,
The agent is the property of the spirit, and not himself;
His self is departed, and he has become the spirit.
The Turk without instruction speaks Arabic; 1
When he returns to himself he knows not a word of it.
Seeing God is lord of spirits and of man,
How can He be inferior in power to a spirit?
When the eagle of alienation from self took wing,
Bayazid began to utter similar speeches;
The torrent of madness bore away his reason,
And he spoke more impiously than before.
"Within my vesture is naught but God,
Whether you seek Him on earth or in heaven."
His disciples all became mad with horror,
And struck with their knives at his holy body.
Each one, like the assassins of Kardkoh, 2
Without fear aimed at the body of his chief.
Each who aimed at the body of the Shaikh,
His stroke was reversed and wounded the striker.
No stroke took effect on that man of spiritual gifts,
But the disciples were wounded and drowned in blood.
Each who had aimed a blow at his neck,
Saw his own throat cut, and gave up the ghost;
He who had struck at his breast
Had cleft his own breast and killed himself.
They who knew better that lord of felicity,
Who had not courage enough to strike a deadly blow,
Their half-knowledge held their hands back;
They saved their lives but slightly wounded themselves.
On the morrow those disciples, diminished in number,

Raised lamentations in their houses.
They went to Bayazid, thousands of men and women,
Saying, "The two worlds are hidden in thy vesture;
If this body of thine were that of a man,
It would have perished of sword-wounds, like a man's."
The man in his senses fought with him 'beside himself,
And thrust the thorn into his own eyes."
Ah! you who smite with your sword him beside himself,
You smite yourself therewith; Beware!
For he that is beside himself is annihilated and safe;
Yea, he dwells in security forever.
His form is vanished, he is a mere mirror;
Nothing is seen in him but the reflection of another.
If you spit at it, you spit at your own face,
And if you hit that mirror, you hit yourself;
And if you see an ugly face in it, 'tis your own,
And if you see an 'Isa there, you are its mother Mary.
He is neither this nor that he is void of form;
'Tis your own form which is reflected back to you.
But when the discourse reaches this point, lip is closed;
When pen reaches this point, it is split in twain.
Close then your lips, though eloquence be possible.
Keep silence; God knows the right way!
This is followed by an anecdote of the Prophet appointing an
Hudhaili youth to be captain of a band of warriors amongst whom
were many older and more experienced soldiers, and of the
objections made to this appointment, and of the Prophet's answer
to the objectors.
Why the Prophet promoted the youth to command his seniors.
The Prophet said, "O ye who regard only the outside,
Regard him not as a youth void of talents.
Many are they whose beards are black yet are old,
Many too have white beards and hearts like pitch.
I have made trial of his wisdom often and often,
And that youth has shown himself old in his actions.
Age consists in maturity of wisdom, O son,

Not, in whiteness of the beard and hair.
How can any one be older than Iblis?
Yet, if he has no wisdom, he is naught.
Suppose him an infant, if he has 'Isa's soul,
He is pure from pride and from carnal lust.
That whiteness of the hair is a sign of maturity
Only to purblind eyes whose vision is limited.
Since that shortsighted one judges by outward signs,
He seeks the right course by outward tokens.
For his sake I said that if ye desire counsel
Ye ought to make choice of an old man.
He who has emerged from the veil of blind belief
Beholds by the light of God all things that exist.
His pure light, without signs or tokens,
Cleaves for him the rind and brings him to the kernel.
To the regarder of externals, genuine and base coin are alike.
How can he know what is inside the basket?
Many are the gold coins made black with smoke,
So that they elude the clutches of greedy thieves;
Many are the copper coins gilded with gold,
And sold as gold to men of slender wits.
We who regard the inside of the world,
We look at the heart and disregard the outside.
The judges who confine their view to externals
And base their decisions on outward appearances,
As they testify and make outward show of faith, 3
Are straightway dubbed faithful by men of externals.
Therefore these heretics, who regard only externals,
Have secretly shed the blood of many true believers.
Strive then to be old in wisdom and in faith,
That, like Universal Reason, you may see within." 4
*NOTES:
1. Alluding to the story of the Kurd, Syad Abul-Wafa, Book i Story
xiv. note.
2. A hill in Mazandaran.
3. "And some there are who say, 'We believe in God and in the last

day,' yet they are not believers" (Koran ii. 7).
4. Universal Reason, here applied to Muhammad. "The first thing which God created was ('aql) Reason or Intelligence," i.e., the Logos.

STORY V.

The Three Fishes.
This story, which is taken from the book of Kalila and Damnah,1 is as follows. There was in a secluded place a lake, which was fed by a running stream, and in this lake were three fishes, one very wise, the second half wise, and the third foolish. One day some fishermen passed by that lake, and having espied the fish, hastened home to fetch their nets. The fish also saw the fishermen and were sorely disquieted. The very wise fish, without a minute's delay, quitted the lake and took refuge in the running stream which communicated with it, and thus escaped the impending danger. The half wise fish delayed doing anything till the fishermen actually made their appearance with their nets. He then floated upon the surface of the water, pretending to be dead, and the fisherman took him up and threw him into the stream, and by this device he saved his life. But the foolish fish did nothing but swim wildly about, and was taken and killed by the fishermen.
The marks of the wise man, of the half wise, and of the fool.
The wise man is he who possesses a torch of his own;
He is the guide and leader of the caravan.
That leader is his own director and light;
That illuminated one follows his own lead.
He is his own protector; do ye also seek protection
From that light whereon his soul is nurtured.
The second, he, namely, who is half wise,
Knows the wise man to be the light of his eyes.
He clings to the wise man like a blind man to his guide,
So as to become possessed of the wise man's sight.

But the fool, who has no particle of wisdom,
Has no wisdom of his own, and quits the wise man.
He knows nothing of the way, great or small,
And is ashamed to follow the footsteps of the guide.
He wanders into the boundless desert,
Sometimes halting and despairing, sometimes running.
He has no lamp wherewith to light himself on his way,
Nor half a lamp which might recognize and seek light.
He lacks wisdom, so as to boast of being alive,
And also half wisdom, so as to assume to be dead?
That half wise one became as one utterly dead
In order to rise up out of his degradation.
If you lack perfect wisdom, make yourself as dead
Under the shadow of the wise, whose words give life.
The fool is neither alive so as to companion with 'Isa,
Nor yet dead so as to feel the power of 'Isa's breath.
His blind soul wanders in every direction,
And at last makes a spring, but springs not upwards.
The counsels of the bird.
A man captured a bird by wiles and snares;
The bird said to him, "O noble sir,
In your time you have eaten many oxen and sheep,
And likewise sacrificed many camels;
You have never become satisfied with their meat,
So you will not be satisfied with my flesh.
Let me go, that I may give you three counsels,
Whence you will see whether I am wise or foolish.
The first of my counsels shall be given on your wrist,
The second on your well-plastered roof,
And the third I will give you from the top of a tree.
On hearing all three you will deem yourself happy.
As regards the counsel on your wrist, 'tis this.
'Believe not foolish assertions of any one!'"
When he had spoken this counsel on his wrist, he flew
Up to the top of the roof, entirely free.
Then he said, "Do not grieve for what is past;

When a thing is done, vex not yourself about it."
He continued, "Hidden inside this body of mine
Is a precious pearl, ten drachms in weight.
That jewel of right, belonged to you,
Wealth for yourself and prosperity for your children.
You have lost it, as it, was not fated you should get it,
That pearl whose like can nowhere be found."
Thereupon the man, like a woman in her travail,
Gave vent to lamentations and weeping.
The bird said to him, "Did I not counsel you, saying,
'Beware of grieving over what is past and gone?'
When 'tis past and gone, why sorrow for it?
Either you understood not my counsel or are deaf.
The second counsel I gave you was this, namely,
'Be not misguided enough to believe foolish assertions.'
O fool, altogether I do not weigh three drachms,
How can a pearl of ten drachms be within me?"
The man recovered himself and said, "Well then,
Tell me now your third good counsel!"
The bird replied, "You have made a fine use of the others,
That I should waste my third counsel upon you.
To give counsel to a sleepy ignoramus
Is to sow seeds upon salt land.
Torn garments of folly and ignorance cannot be patched.
O counselors, waste not the seed of counsel on them!"
*NOTES:
1. Anvar i Suhaili. Book i. Story 15.

STORY VI.

Moses and Pharaoh. 1
Then follows a very long account of the dealings of Moses, an
incarnation of true reason, with Pharaoh, the exponent of mere
opinion or illusion. It begins with a long discussion between Moses
and Pharaoh. Moses tells Pharaoh that both of them alike owe their
bodies to earth and their souls to God, and that God is their only
lord. Pharaoh replies that he is lord of Moses, and chides Moses for
his want of gratitude to himself for nurturing him in his childhood.
Moses replies that he recognizes no lord but God, and reminds
Pharaoh how he had tried to kill him in his infancy. Pharaoh
complains that he is made of no account by Moses, and Moses
retorts that in order to cultivate a waste field it is necessary to break
up the soil; and in order to make a good garment, the stuff must
first be cut up; and in order to make bread, the wheat must first be
ground in the mill, and so on. The best return he can make to
Pharaoh for his hospitality to him in his infancy is to set him free
from his lust-engendered illusions, like a fish from the fish-hook
which has caught him. Pharaoh then twits Moses with his sorceries
in changing his staff into a serpent, and thereby beguiling the
people. Moses replies that all this was accomplished not by sorcery,
like that of Pharaoh's own magicians, but by the power of God,
though Pharaoh could not see it, owing to his want of perception of
divine things. The ear and the nose cannot see beautiful objects,
but only the eye, and similarly the sensual eye, blinded by lust, is
impotent to behold spiritual truth. On the other hand, men of
spiritual insight, whose vision is purged from lust, become as it were
all eyes, and no longer see double, but only the One sole real Being.
Man's body, it is true, is formed of earth, but by discipline and
contrition it may be made to reflect spiritual verities, even as coarse
and hard iron may be polished into a steel mirror. Pharaoh ought to

cleanse the rust of evil-doing from his soul, and then he would be able to see the spiritual truths which Moses was displaying before him. The door of repentance is always open. Moses then promised that if Pharaoh would obey one admonition he should receive in return four advantages. Pharaoh was tempted by this promise, and asked what the admonition was. Moses answered that it was this, that Pharaoh should confess that there is no God except the One Creator of all things in heaven and on earth. Pharaoh then prayed him to expound the four advantages he had promised, saying that possibly they might cure him of infidelity, and cause him to become a vessel of mercy, instead of one of wrath. Moses then explained that they were as follows:

(1) Health.

(2) Long life, ending in the conviction that death is gain.

Even as one who knows of a treasure hid in a ruined house pulls down the house to find that treasure, so does the wise man, full of years and experience, pull down the house of the body to gain the treasure of eternal life. The tradition "I was a hidden treasure," bears on this matter.

(3) A better kingdom than that of Egypt, one of peace in place of one of enmity and contention.

(4) Perpetual youth.

Pharaoh then proceeded to take counsel with his wife, Asiya, whether it would be advisable to quit his infidelity and believe in the promises of Moses. Asiya, being a pious woman and well inclined to Moses, whom she had nurtured in his infancy, urged him to do so, but Pharaoh said he would first consult his vazir Haman. Asiya had a bad opinion of Haman, whom she knew to be as blind to spiritual truths as Pharaoh himself, and she did her best to dissuade Pharaoh from consulting him. To illustrate Haman's spiritual blindness, she told the story of a royal falcon who fell into the hands of an ignorant old woman. This old woman knew nothing of the virtues of a falcon, and was displeased at the falcon's appearance, and said to it, "What was your mother about to leave your claws and beak so long?" She then proceeded to trim them short, according to her fancy, and of course spoiled the falcon for all purposes of falconry. Pharaoh, however, would not be diverted from his purpose of consulting Haman, and Asiya was fain to console herself with the reflection that like always herds with like, and so Pharaoh must needs consort with Haman, who was in so many respects a duplicate of himself. To illustrate this she recalled the story of a woman whose infant had crawled to the brink of a canal, where it persisted in remaining, at the imminent peril of its life, despite all her calls and entreaties. In her distress she asked aid of Ali, who told her to place another infant on the top of the bank. She did so, and her own infant, seeing its playfellow, left the brink of its own accord and came to join its fellow. The spirit of man is of like genus with the holy prophets, but man's animal lust with the demons. And as things of like nature attract one another, so unlike things repel one another. Thus it is said that when holy men pray to be delivered from hell, hell also prays that they may be kept away from it. Pharaoh then proceeded to consult Haman, and Haman, on hearing that Moses had proposed to Pharaoh to humble himself and confess the supreme lordship of Allah, was indignant and rent his clothes, saying, "Is not the kingdom of Egypt thine? Art thou not mightier than this despicable fellow? 2 Who is he to degrade Pharaoh from his 'supreme lordship?'" So Pharaoh listened to Haman and refused to be converted to the true faith. Then Moses was much discouraged, but he was consoled by a voice from heaven assuring him that he was well-beloved of God, because in spite of disappointments and through good and evil he clung to God.

On the tradition, "I was a hidden treasure and I desired to be known, and I created the world in order to be known".

Destroy your house, and with the treasure hidden in it 3
You will be able to build thousands of houses.
The treasure lies under it; there is no help for it;
Hesitate not to pull it down; do not tarry!
For with the coin of that treasure
A thousand houses can be built without labor.
At last of a surety that house will be destroyed,
And the divine treasure will be seen beneath it.

But 'twill not belong to you, because in truth 4
That prize is the wages for destroying the house.
When one has not done the work he gets no wages;
"Man gets nothing he has not worked for." 5
Then you will bite your finger, saying, "Alas!
That bright moon was hidden under a cloud.
I did not do what they told me for my good;
Now house and treasure are lost and my hand is empty."
You have taken your house on lease or hired it;
'Tis not your own property to buy and sell.
As to the term of the lease, it is till your death;
In that term you have to turn it to use.
If before the end of the term of the lease
You omit to derive profit from the house,
Then the owner puts you out of it,
And pulls it down himself to find the gold-mine.
While you are now smiting your head in deep regret,
And now tearing your beard to think of your folly,
Saying, "Alas! that house belonged to me;
I was blind and did not derive profit from it.
Alas! the wind has carried off my dwelling
Forever! 'O misery that rests on slaves!' 6
In that house of mine I saw but forms and pictures;
I was enchanted with that house so fleetin!
I was ignorant of the treasure hidden beneath it,
Otherwise I would have grasped an axe as a perfume.
Ah! if I had administered the justice of the axe,
I should now have been quit of sorrow.
But I fixed my gaze on outward forms,
Like an infant I sported with playthings.
Well said the famous Hakim Sanai,
'Thou art a child; thy house is full of pictures.'
In his divine poem he gives this advice,
'Sweep away the dust from thy house!'"
They who recognize the almighty power of God do not ask where
heaven is or where hell is.

"O Pharaoh, if you are wise, I show you mercy;
But if you are an ass, I give you the stick as an ass.
So I will drive you out of your stable,
Even as I make your head and ears bleed with my stick.
In this stable asses and men alike
Are deprived of peace by your oppressions.
See! I have brought a staff for the purpose of correcting
Every ass who does not prove tractable.
It turns into a serpent in vengeance against you,
Because you have become a serpent in deed and character.
You are an evil serpent, swelled to the size of a hill.
Yet look at the Serpent (constellation) in heaven.
This staff is a foretaste to you of hell,
Saying, 'Ho, take refuge in the light!
Otherwise you will fall into my jaws,
And will find no escape from my clutches!'
This staff even now became a serpent,
So that you need not ask, 'Where is God's hell?'
God makes a hell wheresover He wills;
He makes the very sky a snare and trap for birds.
He produces pains and aches in your teeth,
So that you say, ''Tis a hell and serpent's bite.'
Or again He makes your spittle as honey,
So that you say, ''Tis heaven and wine of Paradise.'
He makes sugar to grow in your mouth,
That you may know the might of the divine decrees.
Therefore, bite not the innocent with your teeth;
Bear in mind the divine stroke that tarries not."
God made the Nile blood to the Egyptians,
He preserved the Israelites from the peril,
That you might know how God discerns
Between the wise and the foolish wayfarers.
The Nile learned of God discernment
When it let the ones through and engulphed the others.
God's mercy made the Nile wise,
His wrath made Cain foolish.

Of His mercy He created wisdom in inanimate things,
And of His wrath He deprived the wise of wisdom.
Of His mercy wisdom accrued to inanimate things,
As a chastisement He took wisdom from the wise.
Here at His command wisdom was shed down like rain,
Whilst there wisdom saw His wrath and fled away.
Clouds and sun, and moon and lofty stars,
All come and go in obedience to His ordinance;
No one of them comes save at His appointed time;
It lingers not behind nor anticipates that time.
Whereas you understood not this secret, the prophets
Have instilled this knowledge into stone and staff;
So that you may infer that other inanimate things
Without doubt resemble in this stones and staves.
The obedience of stone and staff is shown to you,
And informs you of that of other inanimate things.
They cry, "We are all aware of God and obey Him;
We are not destructive by mere fortuitous chance."
Thus you know the water of the Nile when in flood
Made distinction between the Egyptians and the Israelites.
You know the others are wise as earth, who, when cleft,
Knew Qarun and swallowed him up in vengeance.
Or like the moon, who heard the command and hasted
To sever itself into two halves in the sky. 7
Or like the trees and stones, which in all places
Were seen to bow down at the feet of Mustafa.
The arguments between a Sunni and a Materialist 8 (Dahri) decided
by the arbitrament of fire.
Last night a Sunni said, "The world is transitory;
The heavens will pass away; 'God will be the heir.'" 9
A philosopher replied, "How know you they are transitory?
How knows the rain the transitory nature of the cloud?
Are you not a mere mote floating in the sunbeams?
How know you that the sun is transitory?
A mere worm buried in a dung-heap,
How can it know the origin and end of the earth?

In blind belief you have accepted this from your father,
And through folly have clung to it ever since.
Tell me what is the proof of its transitoriness,
Or else be silent and indulge not in idle talk."
The Sunni said, "One day I saw two persons
Engaged in argument on this deep question,
Yea, in dispute and controversy and argument.
At last a crowd was gathered round them.
I proceeded towards that company
To inform myself of the subject of their discourse.
One said, 'This sky will pass away;
Doubtless this building had a builder.'
The other said, 'It is eternal and without period;
It had no builder, or it was its own builder.'
The first said, 'Do you then deny the Creator,
The Bringer of day and night, the Sustainer of men?'
He answered, 'Without proof I will not listen
To what you say; 'tis only based on blind belief.
Go! bring proof and evidence, for never
Will I accept this statement without proof.'
He answered, 'The proof is within my heart,
Yea, my proofs are hidden in my heart.
From weakness of vision you see not the new moon;
If I see it, be not angry with me!'
Much talk followed, and the people were perplexed
About the origin and end of the revolving heavens.
Then the first said, 'O friend, within me is a proof
Which assures me of the transitoriness of the heavens.
I hold it for certain, and the sign of certainty
In him who possesses it is entering into fire.
Know this proof is not to be expressed in speech,
Any more than the feeling of love felt by lovers.
The secret I labor to express is not revealed
Save by the pallor and emaciation of my face.
When the tears course down my cheeks,
They are a proof of the beauty and grace of my beloved.'

The other said, "I take not these for a proof,
Though they may be a proof to common people."
The Sunni said, "When genuine and base coin boast,
Saying, 'Thou art false, I am good and genuine,'
Fire is the test ultimately,
When the two rivals are cast into the furnace."
Accordingly both of them entered the furnace,
Both leapt into the fiery flame;
And the philosopher was burnt to ashes,
But the God-fearing Sunni was made fairer than before.
*NOTES:
1. This story is an expansion of Koran xliii. 50 and following verses, and of Koran xi.
2. See Koran xliii. 50.
3. Compare the Hadis, "Die before you die," i.e., mortify your carnal desires, and you will find spiritual treasure.
4. The Turkish commentator translates ruh by Haqq Yoluna, "for the sake of truth," "in the way of truth." The Lucknow commentator, as usual, shirks the difficulty.
5. Koran liii. 40.
6. Koran xxxvi, 29.
7. Koran liv. 1.
8. Ghazzali divides the ancient Greek philosophers into three classes: Dahriyun, Tabayiun, and Ilahiyun. Schmolders, Ecoles Philosophiques, p. 29.
9. Koran xv. 23.

STORY VII.

The Courtier who quarreled with his Friend for saving his Life.
A king was enraged against one of his courtiers, and drew his sword
to slay him. The bystanders were all afraid to interfere, with the
exception of one who boldly threw himself at the king's feet and
begged him to spare the offender. The king at once stayed his hand,
and laid down his sword, saying, "As you have interceded for him, I
would gladly pardon him, even if he had acted as a very demon. I
cannot refuse your entreaties, because they are the same as my
own. In reality, it is not you who make these entreaties for him, but
I who make them through your mouth. I am the real actor in this
matter and you are only my agent. Remember the text, 'You shot
not when you shot;' 1 you are, as it were, the foam, and I the
mighty ocean beneath it. The mercy you show to this offender is
really shown by me, the king." The offender was accordingly
released and went his way; but, strange to say, he showed no
gratitude to his protector, but, on the contrary, omitted to greet
him when he met him, and in other ways refused to recognize the
favor he had received from him. This behavior excited remark, and
people questioned him as to the cause of his ingratitude to his
benefactor. He replied, "I had offered up my life to the king when
this man intervened. It was a moment when, according to the
tradition, 'I was with God in such a manner that neither prophet nor
angel found entrance along with me,' 2 and this man intruded
between us. I desired no mercy save the king's blows; I sought no
shelter save the king. If the king had cut off my head he would have
given me eternal life in return for it. My duty is to sacrifice my life; it
is the king's prerogative to give life. The night which is made dark as
pitch by the king scorns the brightness of the brightest festal day.
He who beholds the king is exalted above all thoughts of mercy and
vengeance. Of a man raised to this exalted state no description is
possible in this world, for he is hidden in God, and words like
'mercy' and 'vengeance' only express men's partial and weak views

of the matter. It is true 'God taught Adam the names of all things,' 3 but that means the real qualities of things, and not such names as ordinary men use, clad in the dress of human speech. The words and expressions we use have merely a relative truth, and do not unfold absolute truth."

He illustrates this by the reply made to the angel Gabriel by Abraham when he was cast into the fire by Nimrod. 4 Gabriel asked him if he could assist him, and Abraham answered, "No! I have no need of your help." When one has attained union with God he has no need of intermediaries. Prophets and apostles are needed as links to connect ordinary men with God, but he who hears the "inner voice" within him has no need to listen to outward words, even of apostles. Although that intercessor is himself dwelling in God, yet my state is higher and more lovely than his. Though he is God's agent, yet I desire not his intercession to save me from evil sent me by God, for evil at God's hand seems to me good. What seems mercy and kindness to the vulgar seems wrath and vengeance to God-intoxicated saints. God's severity and chastisements serve to exalt his saints, though they make the vulgar more ungodly than before, even as the water of the Nile was pure water to the Israelites, but blood to the Egyptians.

Moses asks the Almighty, "Why hast Thou made men to destroy them?" 5

Moses said, "O Lord of the day of account,
Thou makest forms; wherefore, then, destroyest Thou them?
Thou makest charming forms, both men and women;
Wherefore, then, dost Thou lay them waste?"
God answered, "I know that this query of thine
Proceeds not from negation or vain curiosity.
Otherwise I should chastise and punish thee;
Yea, I should rebuke thee for this question.
But thou seekest to discover in my actions
The ruling principle and the eternal mystery,
In order to inform the people thereof,
And to make 'ripe' every 'raw' person.
Yea, O messenger, thou questionest me that I may reveal

My ways to the people, though thou knowest them.
O Moses, go and sow seed in the ground
In order to do justice to this question."
When Moses had sowed and his seed had grown up,
He took a sickle and reaped the corn,
And then a divine voice reached his ears:
"Why hast thou sown and nurtured the corn,
And then cut it down directly it was ripe?"
Moses replied, "Lord, I cut it and lay it low
Because here I have grain and straw.
Grain is out of place in the straw-yard,
And straw is useless in the wheat-barn.
'Tis wrong to mix these two,
It is needful to sift them one from the other."
God said, "From whom learnest thou this knowledge
Whereby thou hast constructed a threshing-floor?"
Moses said, "O Lord, Thou hast given me discernment."
God said, "Then have not I also discernment?
Amongst my creatures there are pure spirits,
And also dark and befouled spirits.
The oyster-shells are not all of the same value;
Some contain pearls, and others black stones.
It is needful to discern the bad from the good,
Just as much as to sift wheat from straw.
The people of this world exist in order to manifest
And to disclose the 'hidden treasure.'
Read, 'I was a hidden treasure, and desired to be known;
Hide not the hidden treasure, but disclose it.
Your true treasure is hidden under a false one,
Just as butter is hidden within the substance of milk.
The false one is this transitory body of yours,
The true one your divine soul.
Long time this milk is exposed to view,
And the soul's butter is hidden and of no account.
Stir up your milk assiduously with knowledge,
So that what is hidden in it may be disclosed;

Because this mortal is the guide to immortality,
As the cries of revellers indicate the cup-bearer."
*NOTES:
1. Koran viii. 17.
2. See Gulshan i Raz, I. 120.
3. Koran ii. 29.
4. See Koran xxi. 68, and the Commentators thereon.
5. So Job x. 8: " Thy hands have made me, yet Thou dost destroy me."

STORY VIII.

The Prince who, after having been beguiled by
a Courtesan, returned to his True Love.

A certain king dreamed that his dearly beloved son, a youth of great promise, had come to an untimely end. On awaking he was rejoiced to find that his son was still alive; but he reflected that an accident might carry him off at any moment, and therefore decided to marry him without delay, in order that the succession might be secured. Accordingly he chose the daughter of a pious Darvesh as a bride for his son, and made preparations for the wedding. But his wife and the other ladies of his harem did not approve of the match, considering it below the dignity of the prince to marry the daughter of a beggar. The king rebuked them, saying that a Darvesh who had renounced worldly wealth for the sake of God was not to be confounded with an ordinary beggar, and insisted on the consummation of the marriage. After the marriage the prince refused to have anything to do with his bride, though she was very fair to look on, and he carried on an intrigue with an ugly old woman who had bewitched him by sorcery. After a year, however, the king found some physicians who succeeded in breaking the spell, and the prince returned to his senses, and his eyes were opened to the superior attractions of his wife, and he renounced his ugly paramour and fell in love with his wife. This is a parable, the true wife being the Deity, the old paramour the world, and the physicians the prophets and saints. Another illustration is a child who played at besieging a mimic fort with his fellows, and succeeded in capturing it and keeping the others out. At this moment God "bestowed on him wisdom, though a child," [1] and it became to him a day "when a man flees from his brethren," [2] and he recognized the emptiness of this idle sport, and engaged in the pursuit of holiness and piety. This is followed by an anecdote of a

45

devotee who had so concentrated his thoughts on things above that he was utterly careless of all earthly troubles, and was cheerful and rejoicing even in the midst of a severe famine.

The world is the outward form of "Universal Reason" (Muhammad), and he who grieves him must expect trouble in the world. 3

The whole world is the outward form of Universal Reason,
For it is the father of all creatures of reason.
When a man acts basely towards Universal Reason,
Its form, the world, shows its teeth at him.
Be loyal to this father and renounce disobedience,
That this earthy house may furnish you golden carpets.
Then the judgment-day will be the "cash of your state,"
Earth and heavens will be transfigured before you. 4
I am ever in concord with this father of ours,
And earth ever appears to me as a Paradise.
Each moment a f1~esh form, a new beauty,
So that weariness vanishes at these ever-fresh sights.
I see the world filled with blessings,
Fresh waters ever welling up from new fountains.
The sound of those waters reaches my ears,
My brain and senses are intoxicated therewith.
Branches of trees dancing like fair damsels,
Leaves clapping hands like singers.
These glories are a mirror shining through a veil;
If the mirror were unveiled, how would it be?
I tell not one in a thousand of them,
Because every ear is stopped with doubt.
To men of illusions these tales are mere good tidings,
But men of knowledge deem them not tidings, but ready cash.

This is illustrated by an anecdote of Ezra or 'Uzair and his sons.5 On his return from Babylon, whither he had been carried captive by Nebuchadnezzar, Ezra beheld the ruins of Jerusalem, and he said, "How shall God give life to this city after it hath been dead?" And God caused him to die for a hundred years, and then raised him again to life, and said to him, "How long hast thou waited?" He said, "I have waited a day." God said, "Nay, thou hast waited a hundred years. Look at the dead bones of thine ass; we will raise them and clothe them with flesh." Ezra was raised from the dead as a young man, whereas his sons were then, of course, very old men. They met him, and asked if he had seen their father. He replied, "I have seen him; he is coming." Some of them rejoiced, considering this good news; but others, who had loved him more dearly, knew him and fainted with joy. What was mere good tidings to the men of opinion was the "ready money of their state" to men of real knowledge.

*NOTES:

1. Koran xix. 13.

2. Koran lxxx. 34.

3. "Aql i Kull, Universal Reason, or the Logos, was identified with the prophet Muhammad."

4. Koran xiv. 49.

5. This story comes from Koran ii. 261.

STORY IX.

The Mule and the Camel.
A mule said to a camel, "How is it that I am always stumbling and falling down, whilst you never make a false step?" The camel replied, "My eyes are always directed upwards, and I see a long way before me, while your eyes look down, and you only see what is immediately under your feet." The mule admitted the truth of the camel's statement, and besought him to act as his guide in future, and the camel consented to do so. Just so partial reason cannot see beyond the grave, but real reason looks onward to the day of judgment, and, therefore, is enabled to steer a better course in this world. For this cause, men having only partial reason or mere opinion of their own ought to follow the guidance of the saints, according to the text, "O believers, enter not upon any affair ere God and his Apostle lead the way." 1
Then follows another anecdote of an Egyptian who asked an Israelite to draw water for him from the Nile, because the water of the Nile turned to blood when drawn by an Egyptian. Afterwards the Egyptian asked the Israelite to pray for him, and the Israelite admonished him to renounce his egotism and conceit of his own existence, which blinded his eyes to divine verities. In illustration of this he tells the same story of an adulterous woman, which is known as the "Merchant's Tale" in Chaucer. This woman, desiring to carry on an intrigue with her paramour, climbed up a pear-tree to gather the fruit, and when she had reached the top she looked down, and pretended that she saw her husband misconducting himself with another woman. The husband assured her there was no one but himself there, and desired her to come down and see for herself. She came down and admitted there was no one there. Her husband then, at her request, ascended the tree, and she at once called her paramour, and began to amuse herself with him.

48

Her husband saw her from his post in the tree, and began to abuse her; but she declared there was no man with her, and that the pear-tree made her husband see double, just as it had made her see double previously.

The evolution of man.

First he appeared in the class of inorganic things, 2
Next he passed therefrom into that of plants.
For years he lived as one of the plants,
Remembering naught of his inorganic state so different;
And when he passed from the vegetive to the animal state
He had no remembrance of his state as a plant,
Except the inclination he felt to the world of plants,
Especially at the time of spring and sweet flowers.
Like the inclination of infants towards their mothers,
Which know not the cause of their inclination to the breast,
Or the excessive inclination of young disciples
Towards their noble and illustrious teachers.
The disciple's partial reason comes from that Reason,
The disciple's shadow is from that bough.
When the shadows in the disciples cease,
They know the reason of their attachment to the teachers.
For, O fortunate one, how can the shadow move,
Unless the tree that casts the shadow move as well?
Again, the great Creator, as you know,
Drew man out of the animal into the human state.
Thus man passed from one order of nature to another,
Till he became wise and knowing and strong as he is now.
Of his first souls he has now no remembrance,
And he will be again changed from his present soul.
In order to escape from his present soul full of lusts
He must behold thousands of reasonable souls.
Though man fell asleep and forgot his previous states,
Yet God will not leave him in this self-forgetfulness;
And then he will laugh at his own former state
Saying, " What mattered my experiences when asleep?
When I had forgotten my prosperous condition,

And knew not that the grief and ills I experienced
Were the effect of sleep and illusion and fancy?
In like manner this world, which is only a dream.
Seems to the sleeper as a thing enduring for ever
But when the morn of the last day shall dawn,
The sleeper will escape from the cloud of illusion;
Laughter will overpower him at his own fancied grieves
When he beholds his abiding home and place.
Whatever you see in this sleep, both good and evil,
Will all be exposed to view on the resurrection day.
Whatever you have done during your sleep in the world
Will be displayed to you clearly when you awake.
Imagine not that these ill deeds of yours exist not
In this sleep of yours, and will not be revealed to you.
But your present laughter will turn to weeping and woe
On the day of revealing, O you who oppress captives!
Your present wailing and sorrow and grieves,
On the other hand, will be joy when you awake,
O you, who have rent the garments of many Josephs,
You will rise from your heavy sleep as a wolf.
Your bad qualities will rise in the shape of wolves
And rend you limb from limb in vengeance.
By the law of retaliation blood sleeps not after death;
Say not, "I shall die and obtain pardon."
The retaliation of this world is illusive,
It is mere sport compared to the retaliation to come.
Therefore God calls the world "a pastime and a sport," 3
For punishment in this world is sport compared to that.
Here punishment is as the repression of quarrels,
There it is as castration or circumcision.

But this discourse is endless, O Moses,
Go and leave these asses to their grazing!
Let them fatten themselves with the food they love,
For they are very wolves and objects of my wrath.

Zu'l Qarnain at Mount Qaf. 4

Zu'l Qarnain journeyed to Mount Qaf;
He saw it was formed of a bright emerald,
Forming as it were a ring round the world,
Whereat all people are filled with wonder.
He said, "Thou mighty hill, what are other hills?
Before thee they are mere playthings."
The Mount replied, "Those hills are my veins,
But they are not like me in beauty and importance.
A hidden vein from me runs to every city,
The quarters of the world are bound to my veins.
When God desires an earthquake under any city,
He bids me shake one of my veins.
Then in anger I shake that vein
Which is connected with that particular city.
When He says, 'Enough,' my vein remains still,
I remain still, and then haste to perform my work.
Now still like a plaster, and now operating;
Now still like thought, and then speaking my thought.
But they who are void of reason imagine
That these earthquakes proceed from earth's vapors."

Just so an ant who saw a pen writing on paper,
Delivered himself to another ant in this way
'That pen is making very wonderful figures,
Like hyacinths and lilies and roses.'
The other said, 'The finger is the real worker,
The pen is only the instrument of its working.'
A third ant said, ' No; the action proceeds from the arm,
The weak finger writes with the arm's might.'
So it went on upwards, till at last
A prince of the ants, who had some wit
Said, 'Ye regard only the outward form of this marvel,
Which form becomes senseless in sleep and death.
Form is only as a dress or a staff in the hand,

It is only from reason and mind these figures proceed.'
But he knew not that this reason and mind
Would be but lifeless things without God's impulse.
The angel Gabriel appears to the Prophet Muhammad.
Mustafa said to the angel Gabriel,
"O friend, show me thy form as it really is;
Show it to me openly and perceptibly,
That I may behold thee with my eyes."
Gabriel said, "Thou canst not do so, thou art too weak,
Thy senses are exceeding weak and frail."
Muhammad said, "Show it, that this body of mine may see
To what extent its senses are frail and impotent.
True, man's bodily senses are frail,
But he possesses within him a mighty property. 5
This body resembles flint and steel,
But like them it has the power of kindling fire.
Flint and steel are able to generate fire,
From them springs fire which can destroy its parents."
As he continued importuning him, Gabriel displayed
His awful form, whereat the mountains were rent asunder.
It occupied the sky from east to west.
And Mustafa swooned with fear.
When Gabriel beheld him swooning with fear,
He came and clasped him in his arms.
Address to Husamu-'d-Din.
O light of God, Husamu-'d-Din, admit
This ass's head into that melon-garden!
For when this ass is killed in the slaughter-house
That kitchen will bestow upon him a new existence.
From me proceeds the form, from thee the spirit;
Nay, form and spirit both proceed from thee!
Thou art as Muhammad in heaven, O brilliant Sun!
Be also as Muhammad on earth forever and ever!
So that earth and heaven on high may be united
With one heart, one worship, one aspiration!
And schism and polytheism and duality disappear,

And Unity abide in the Real Spiritual Being!
When my spirit recognizes thy spirit,
We remember our essential union and origin.

End of the book.